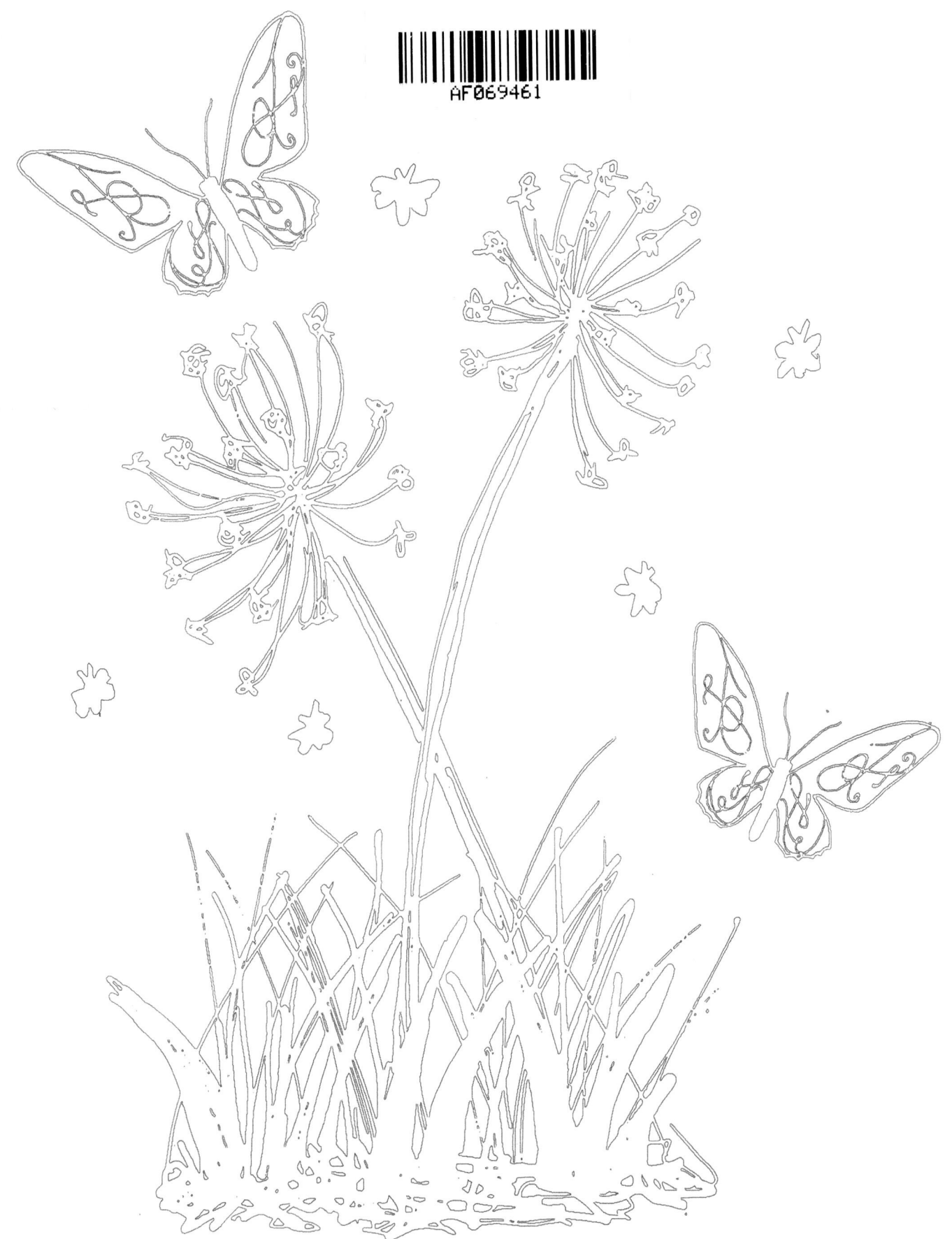

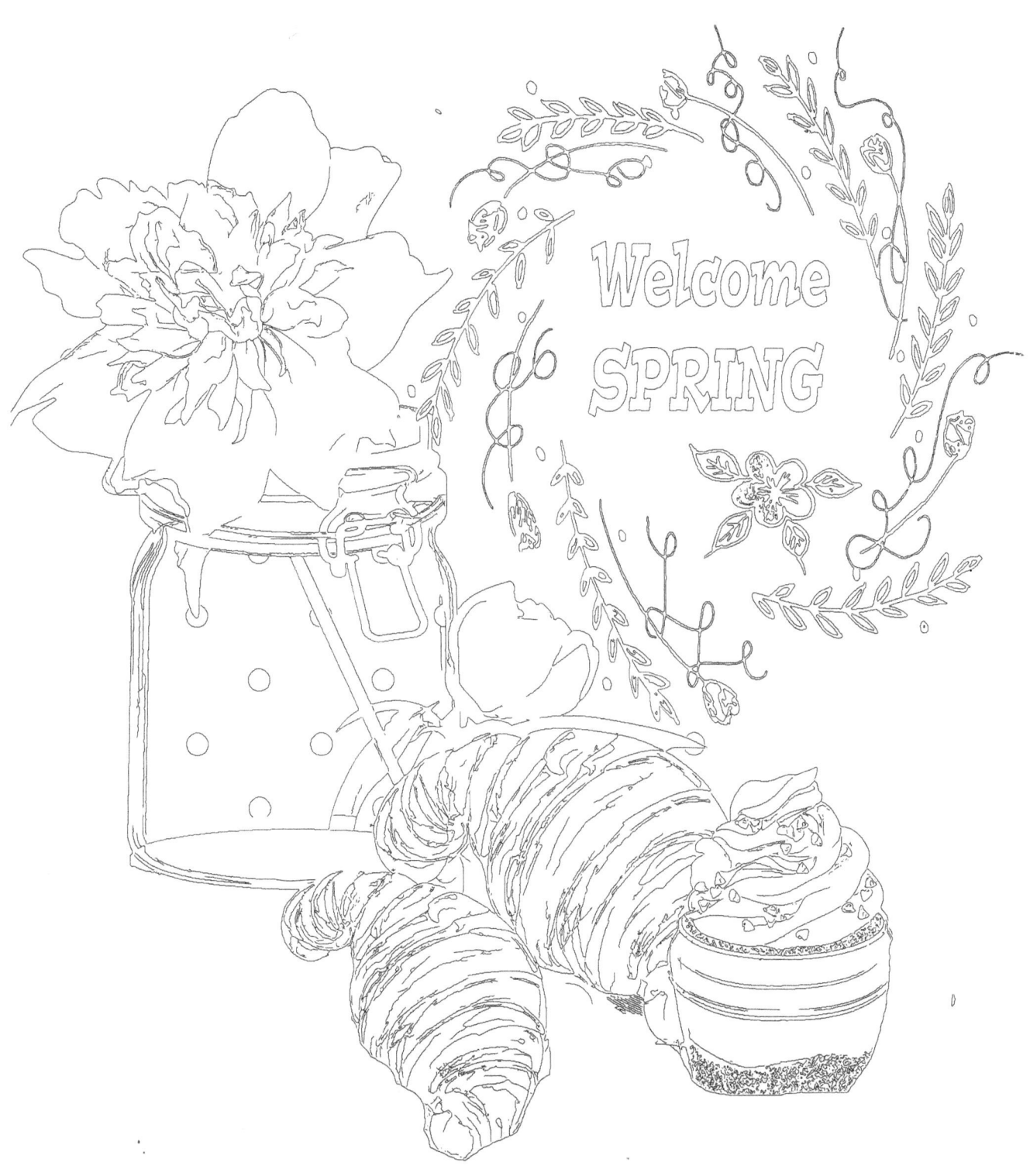

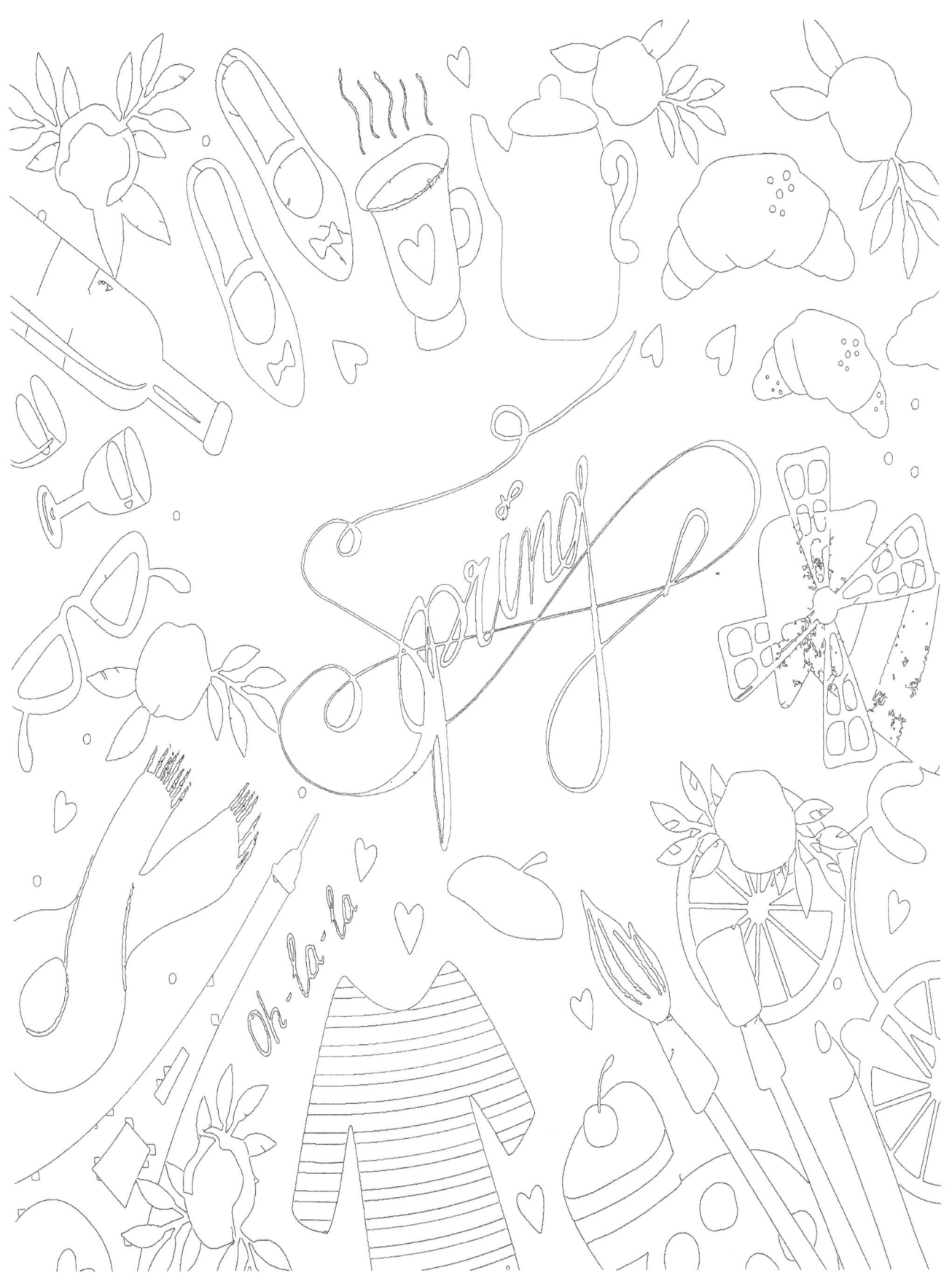

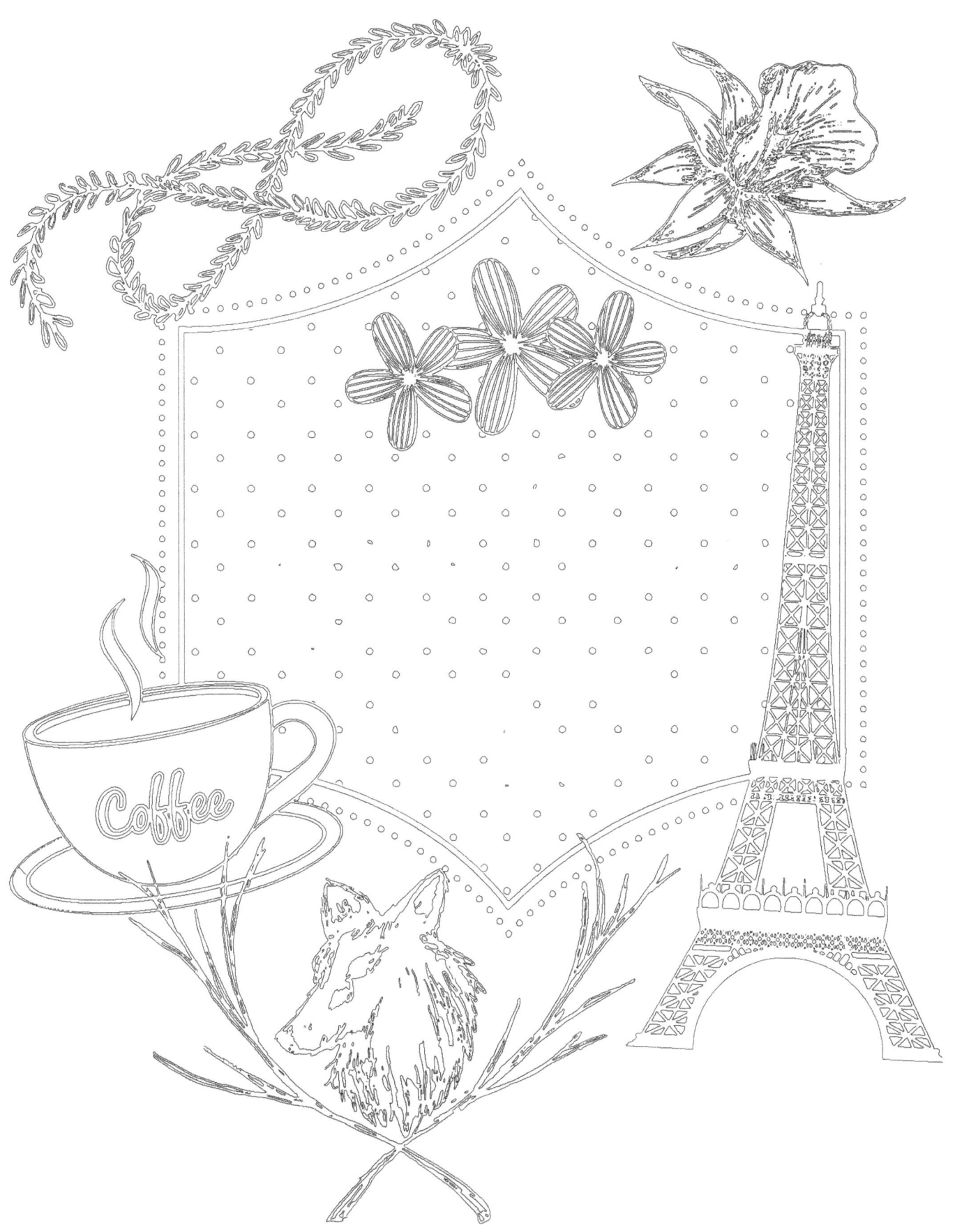

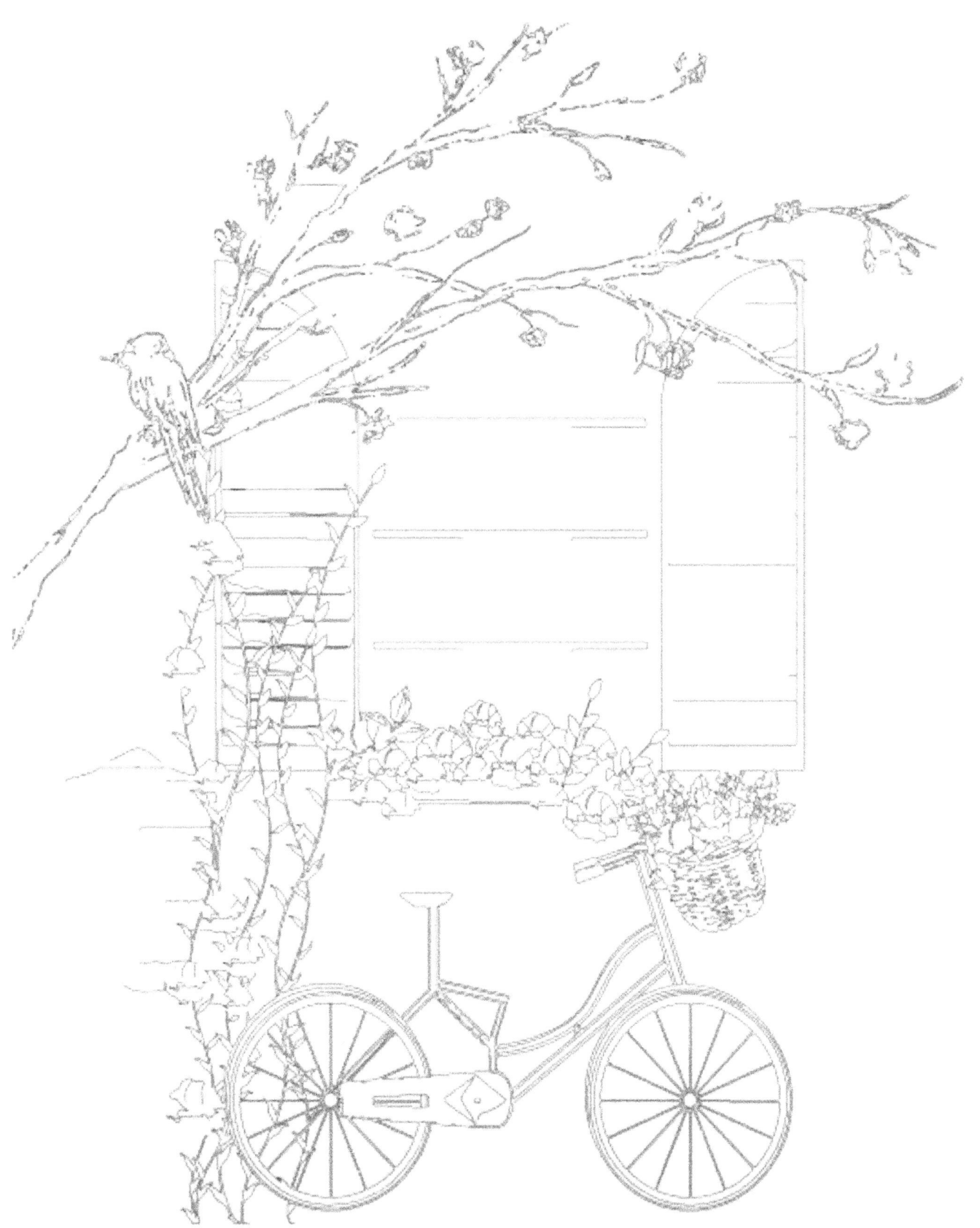

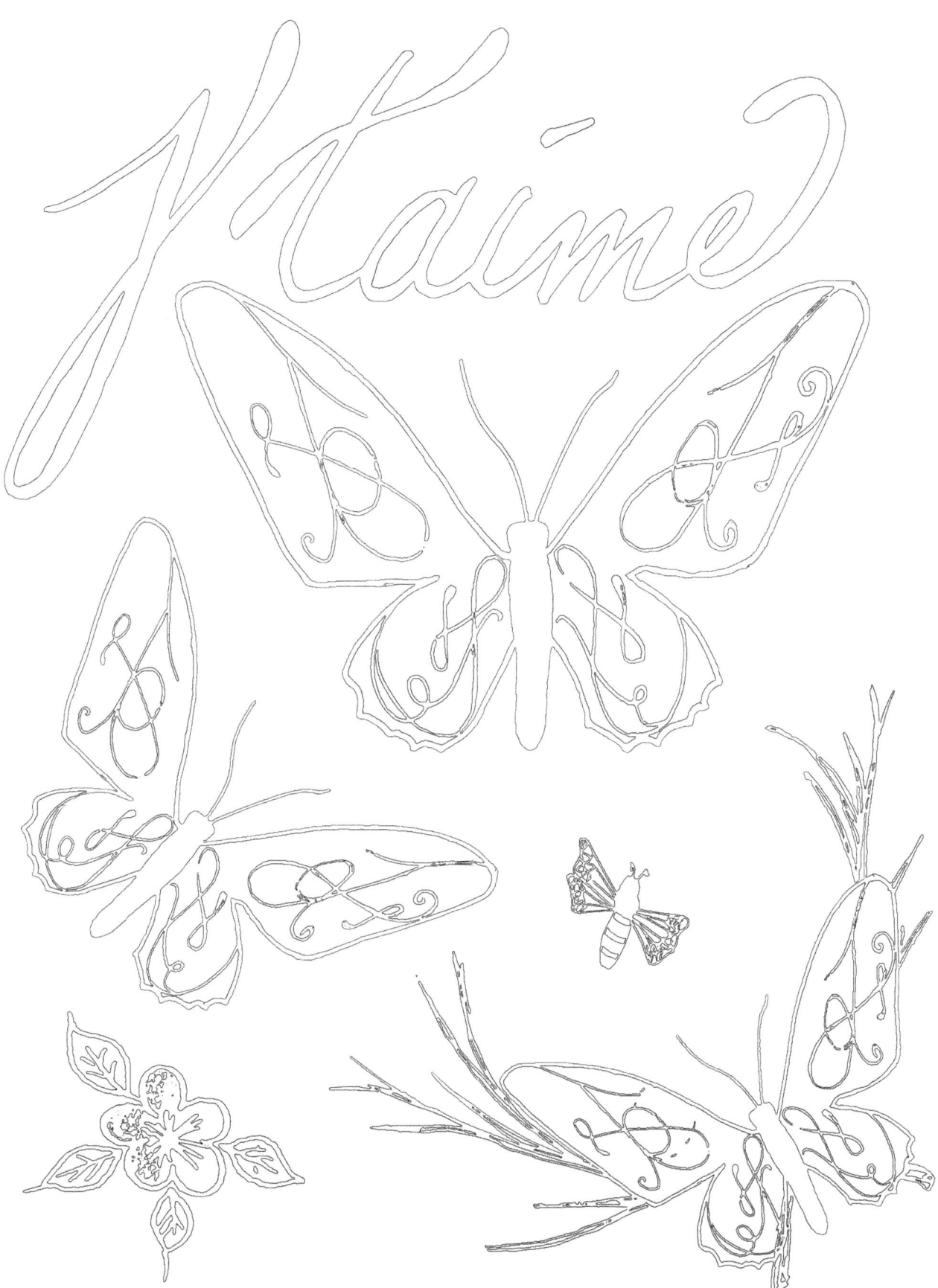

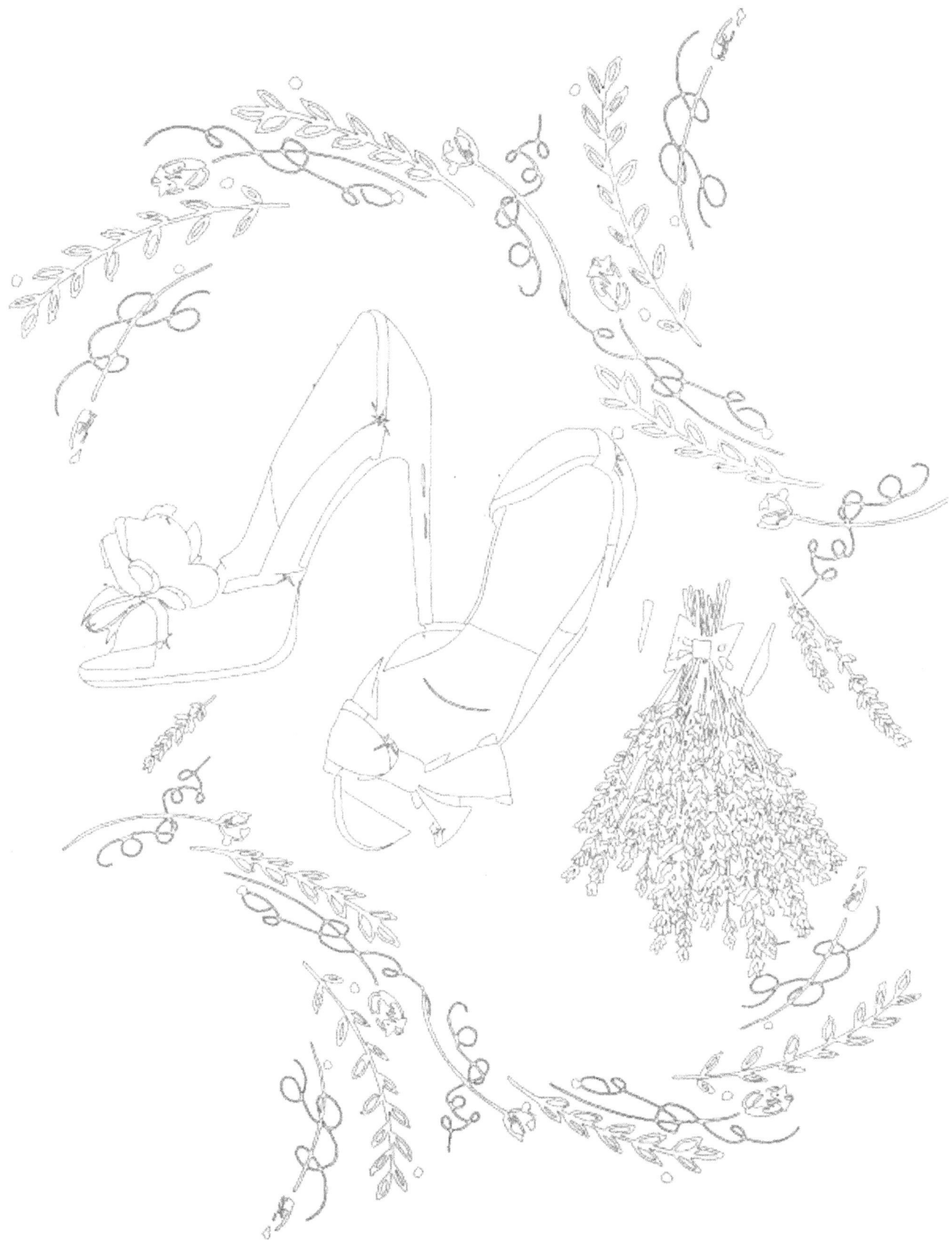

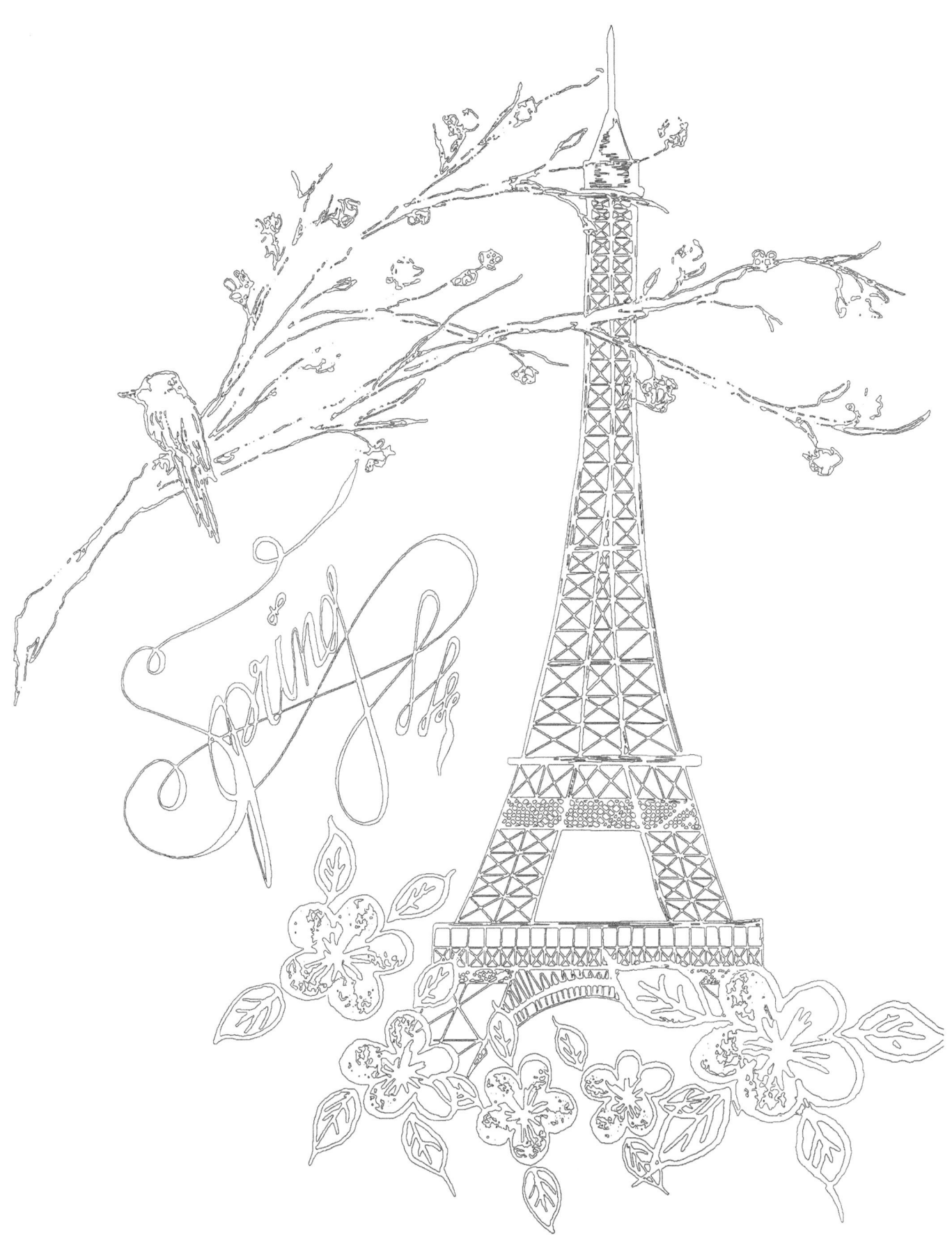

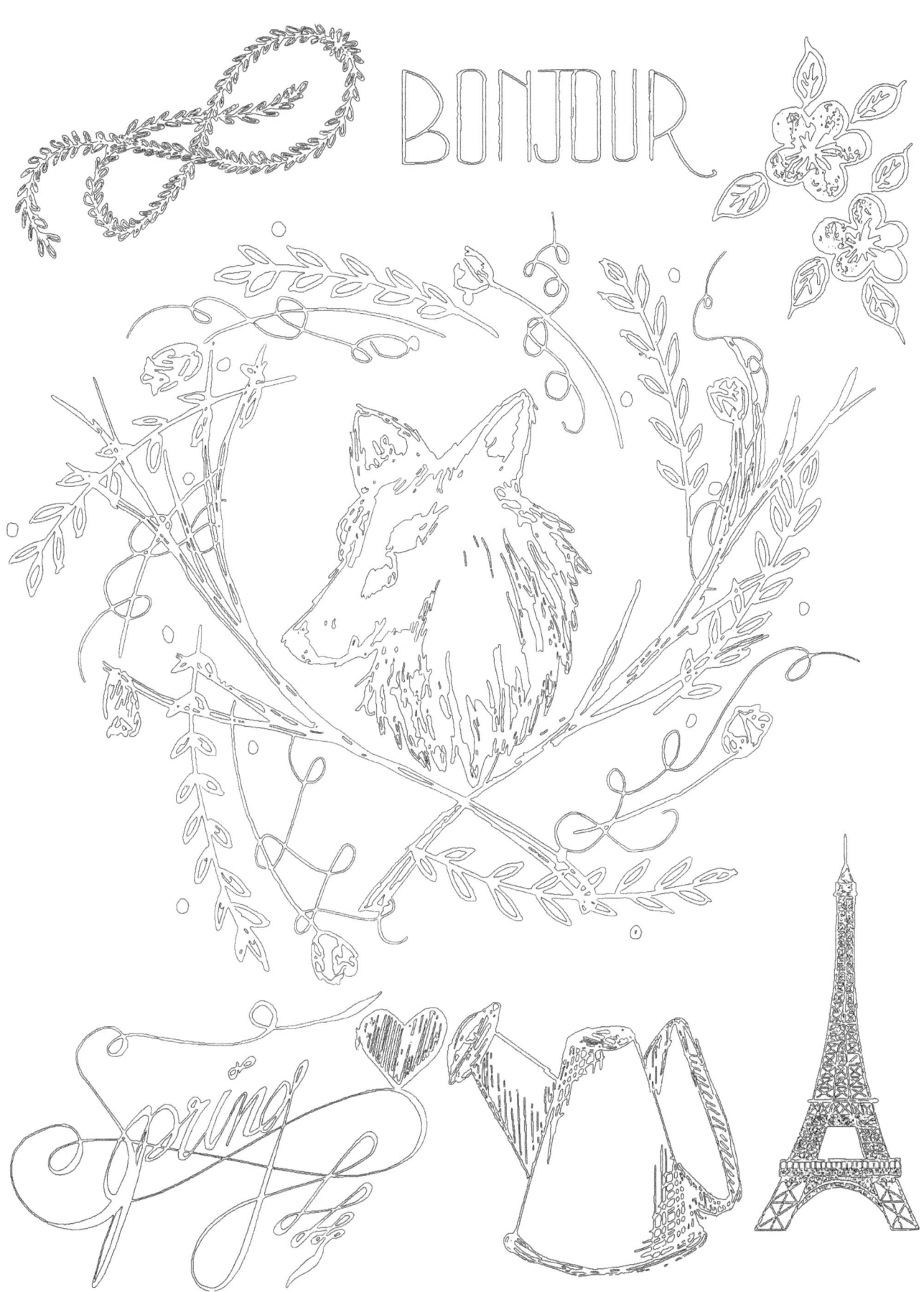

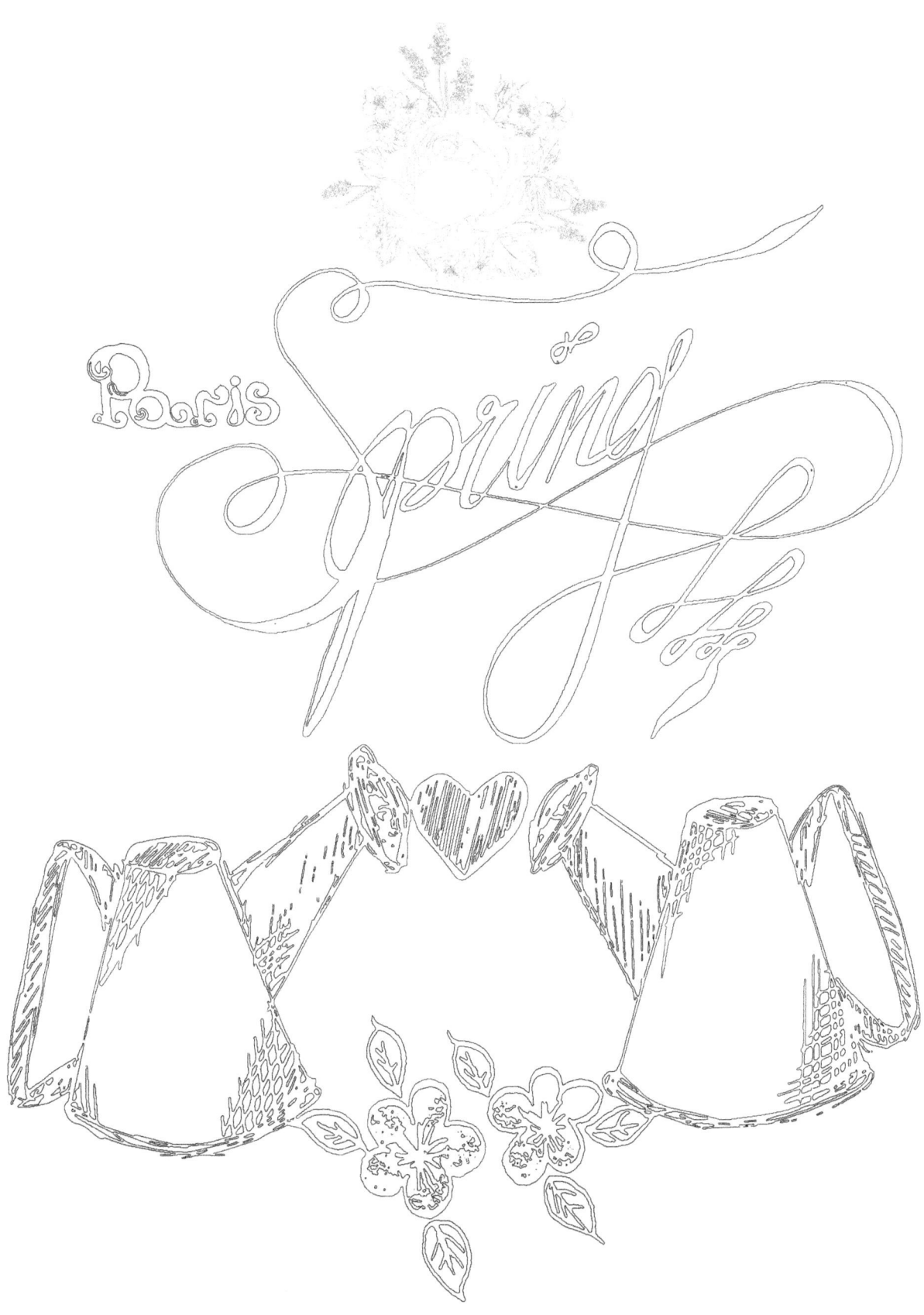

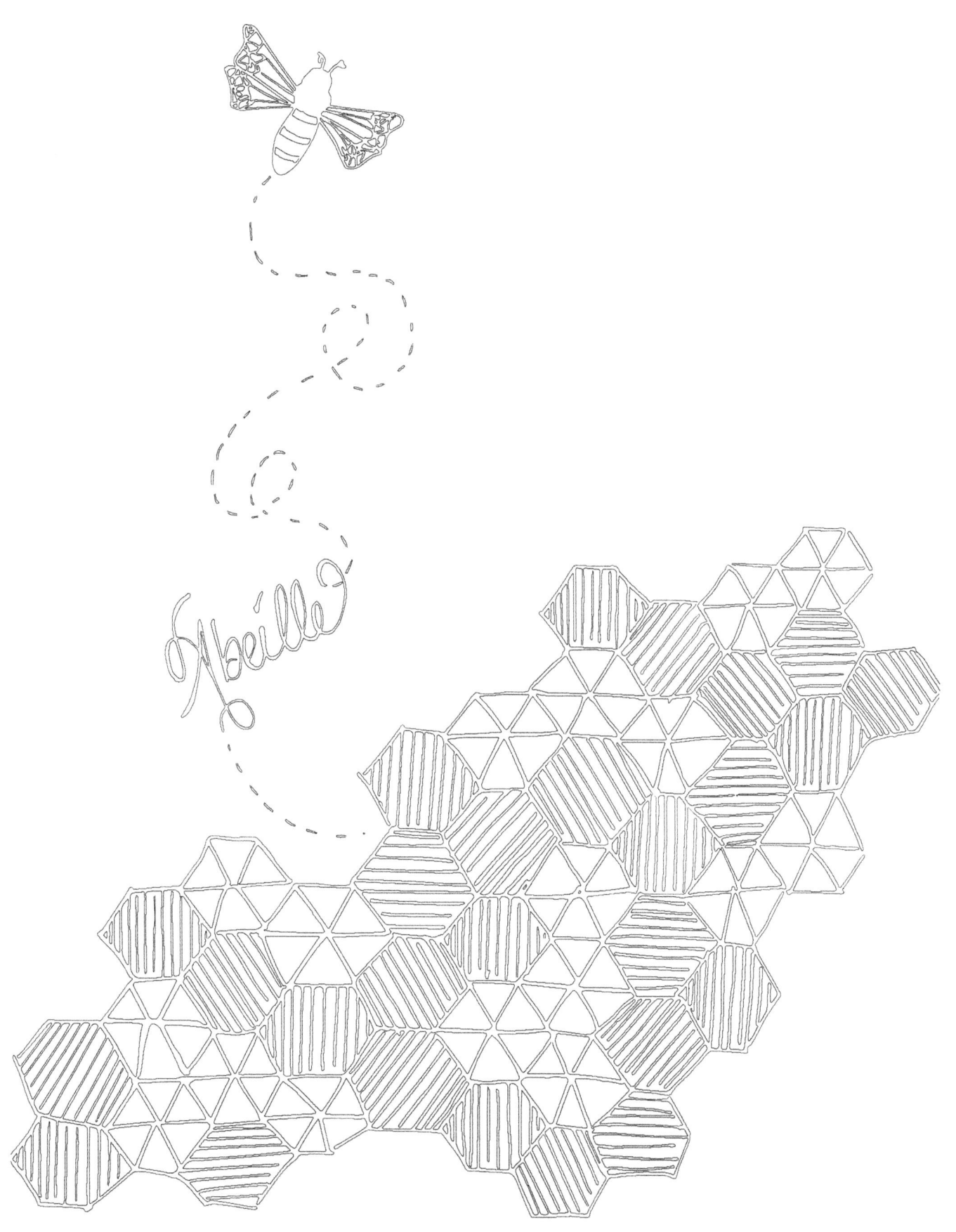

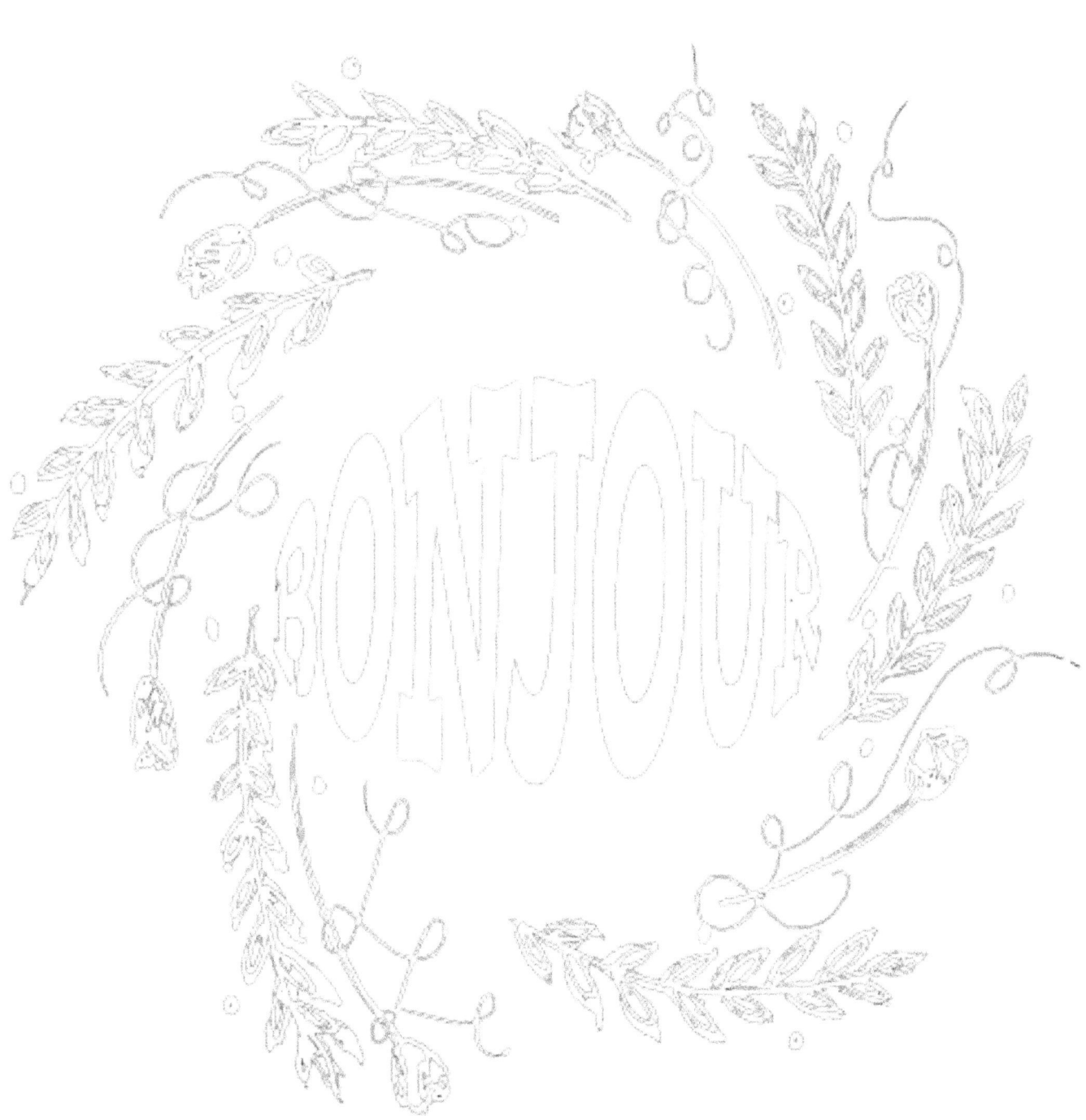

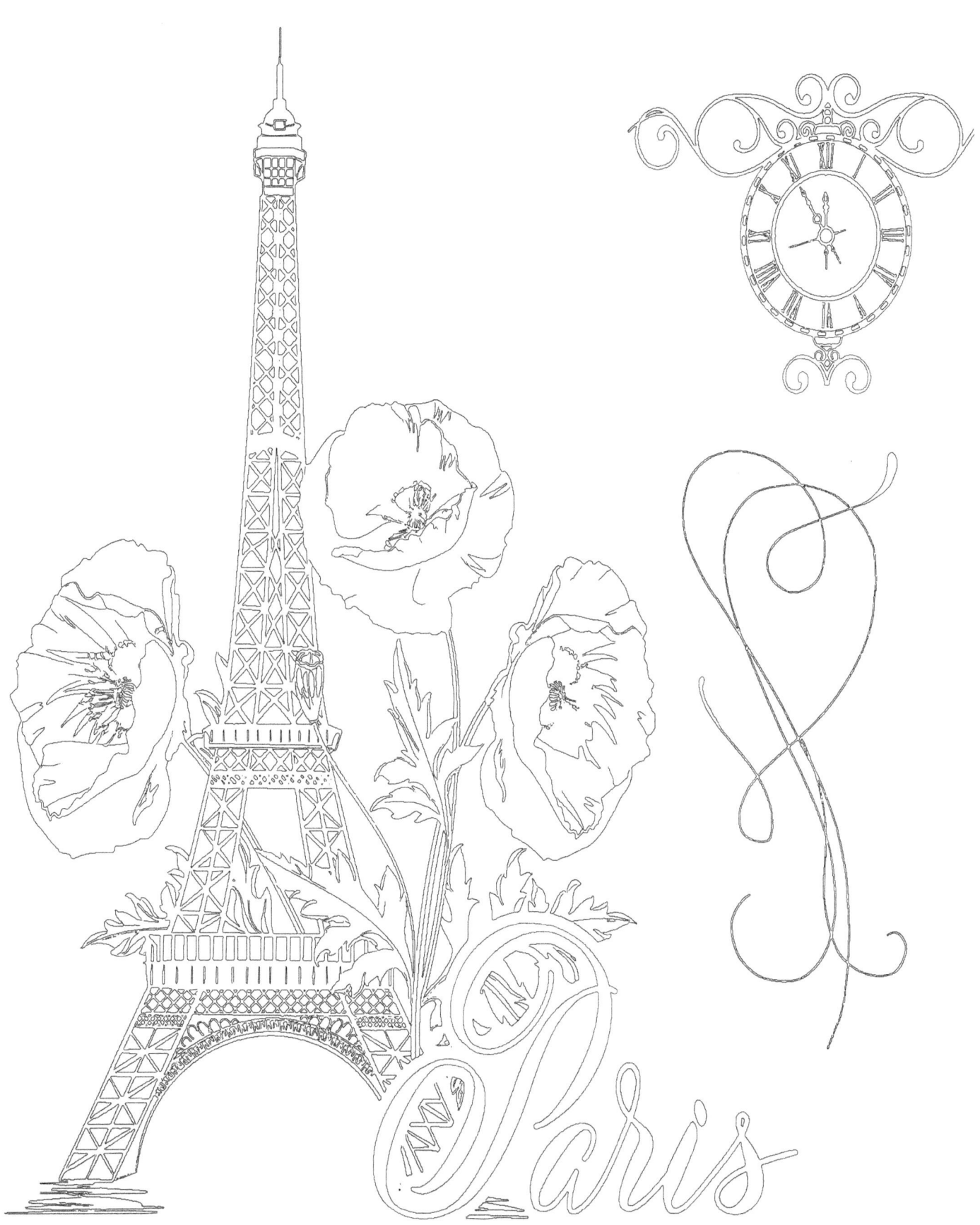

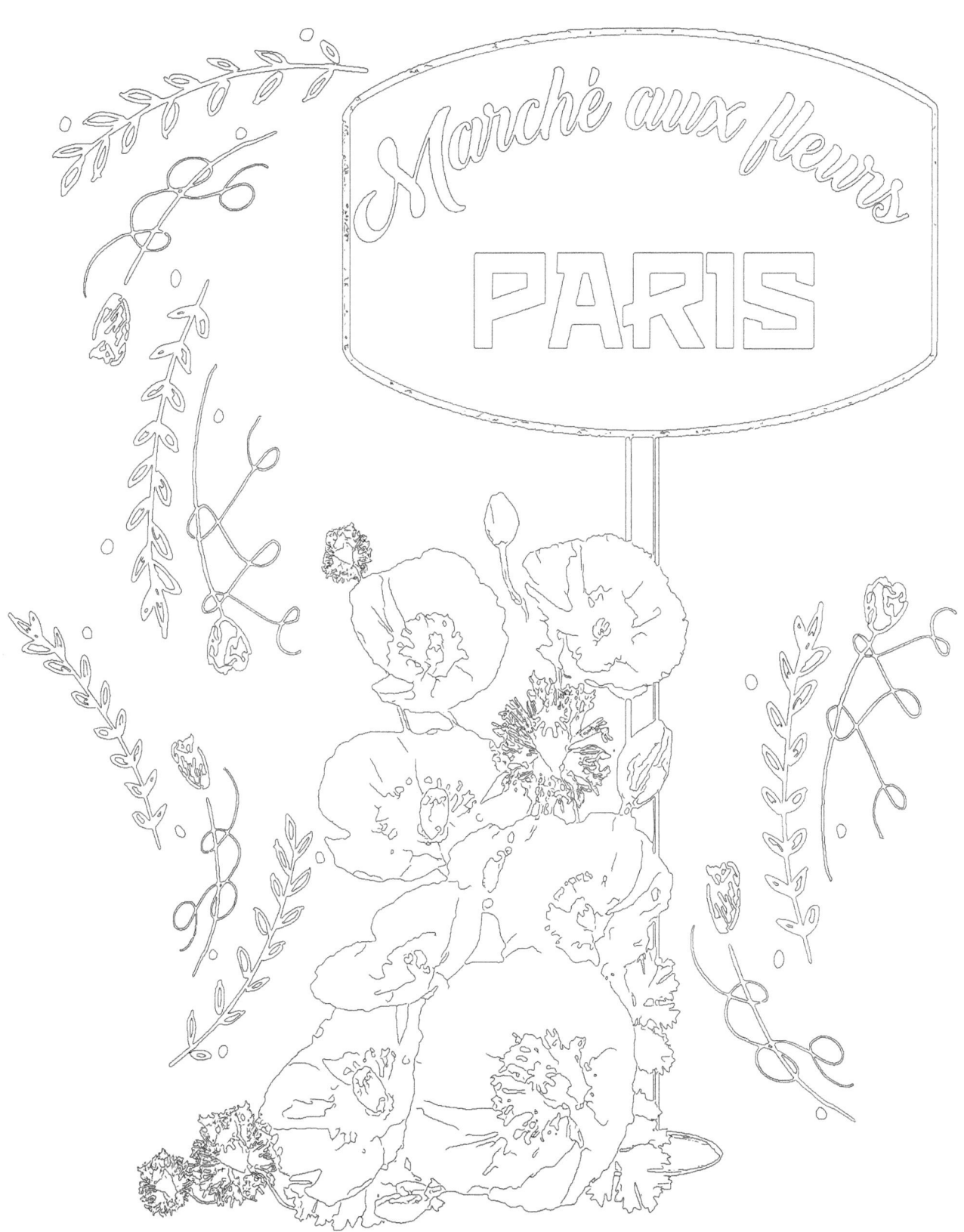

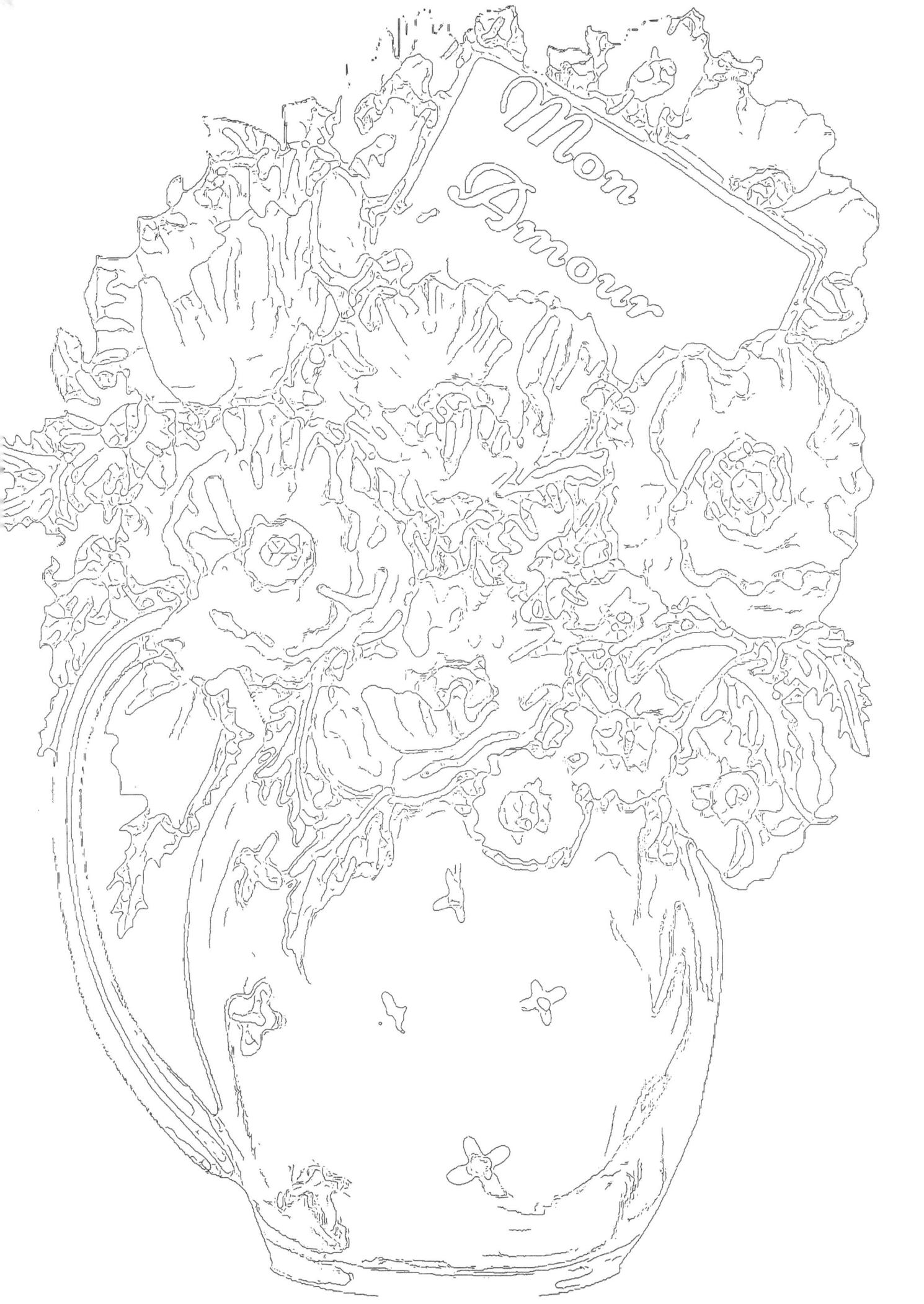

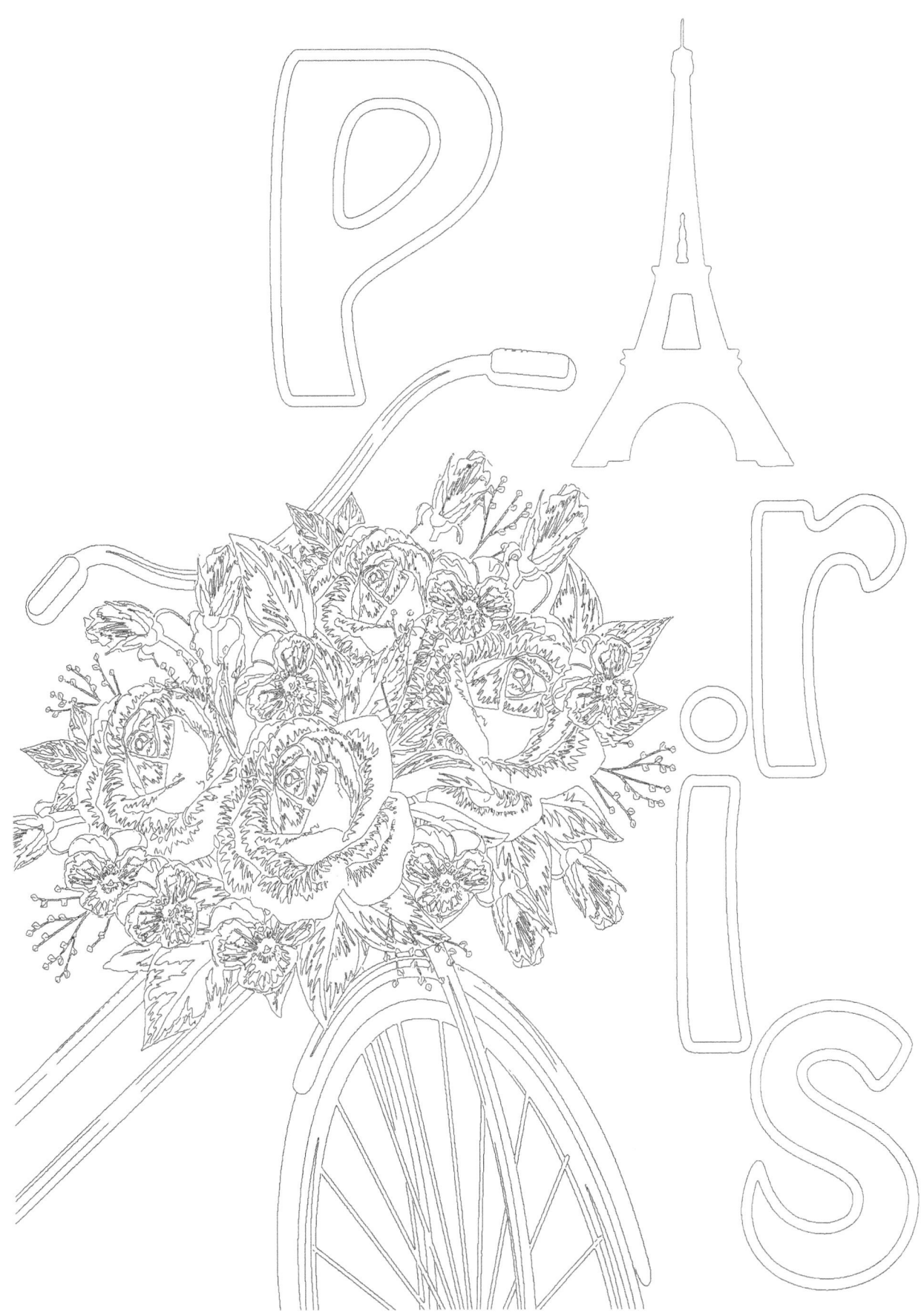

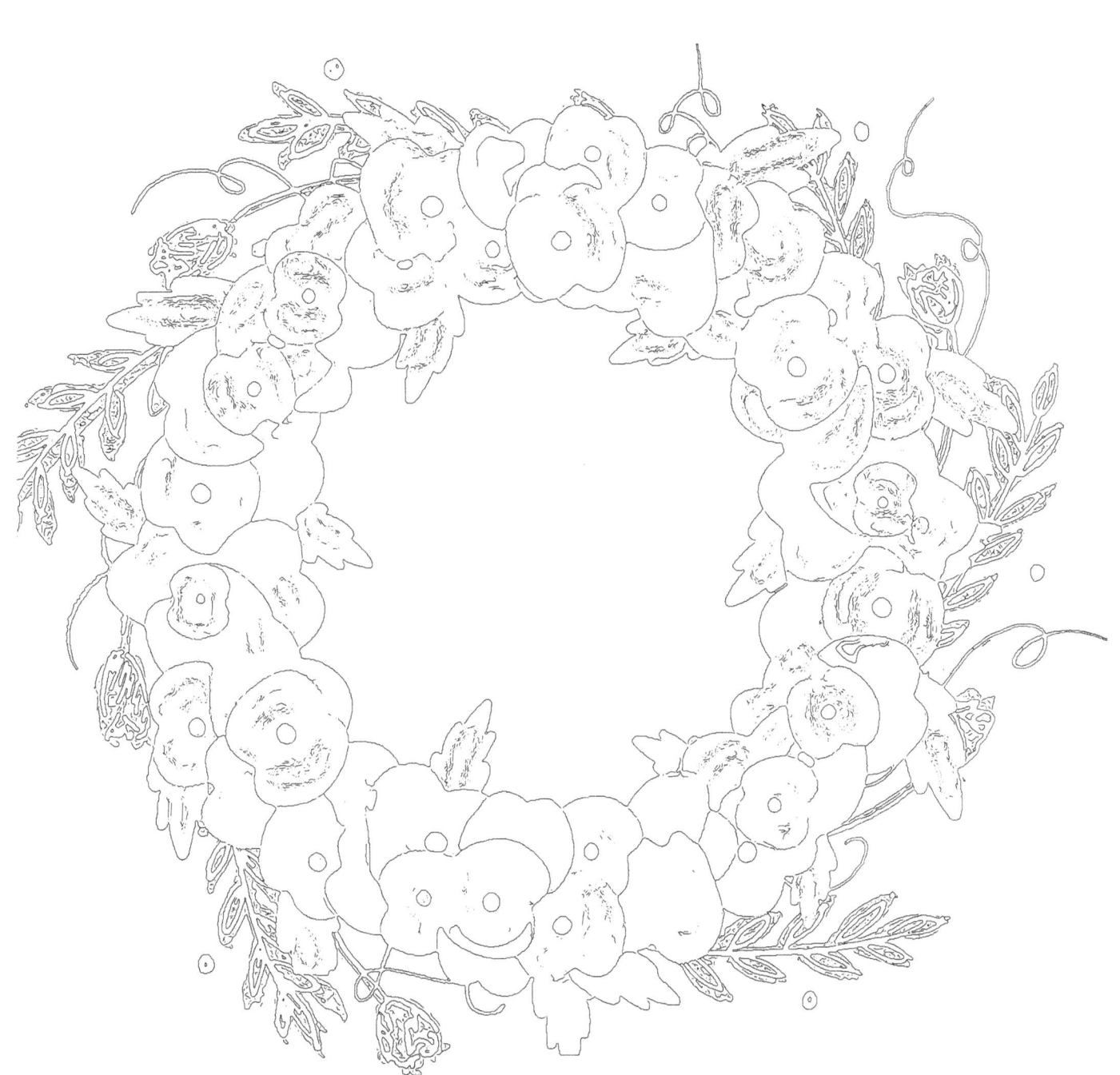

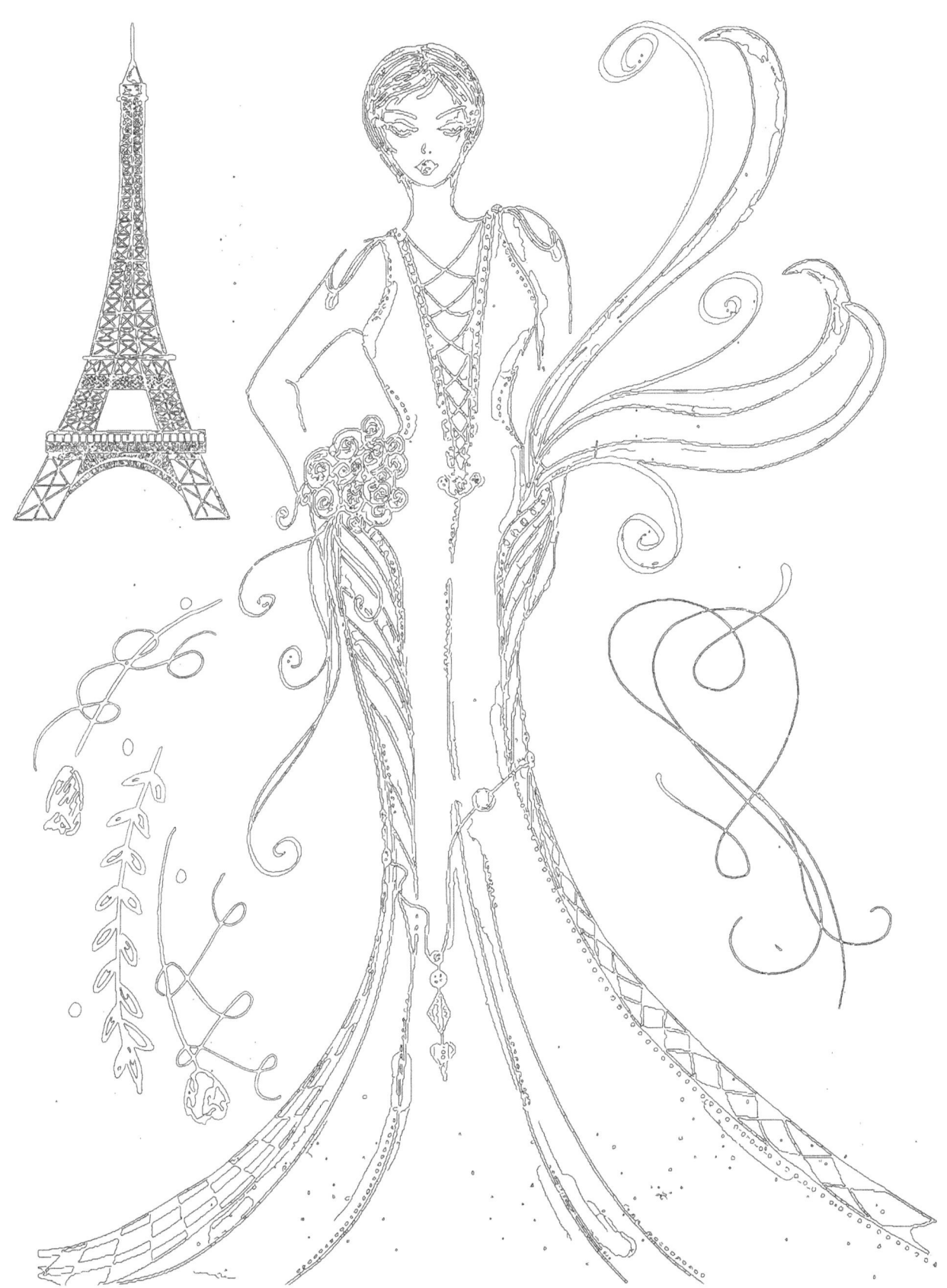

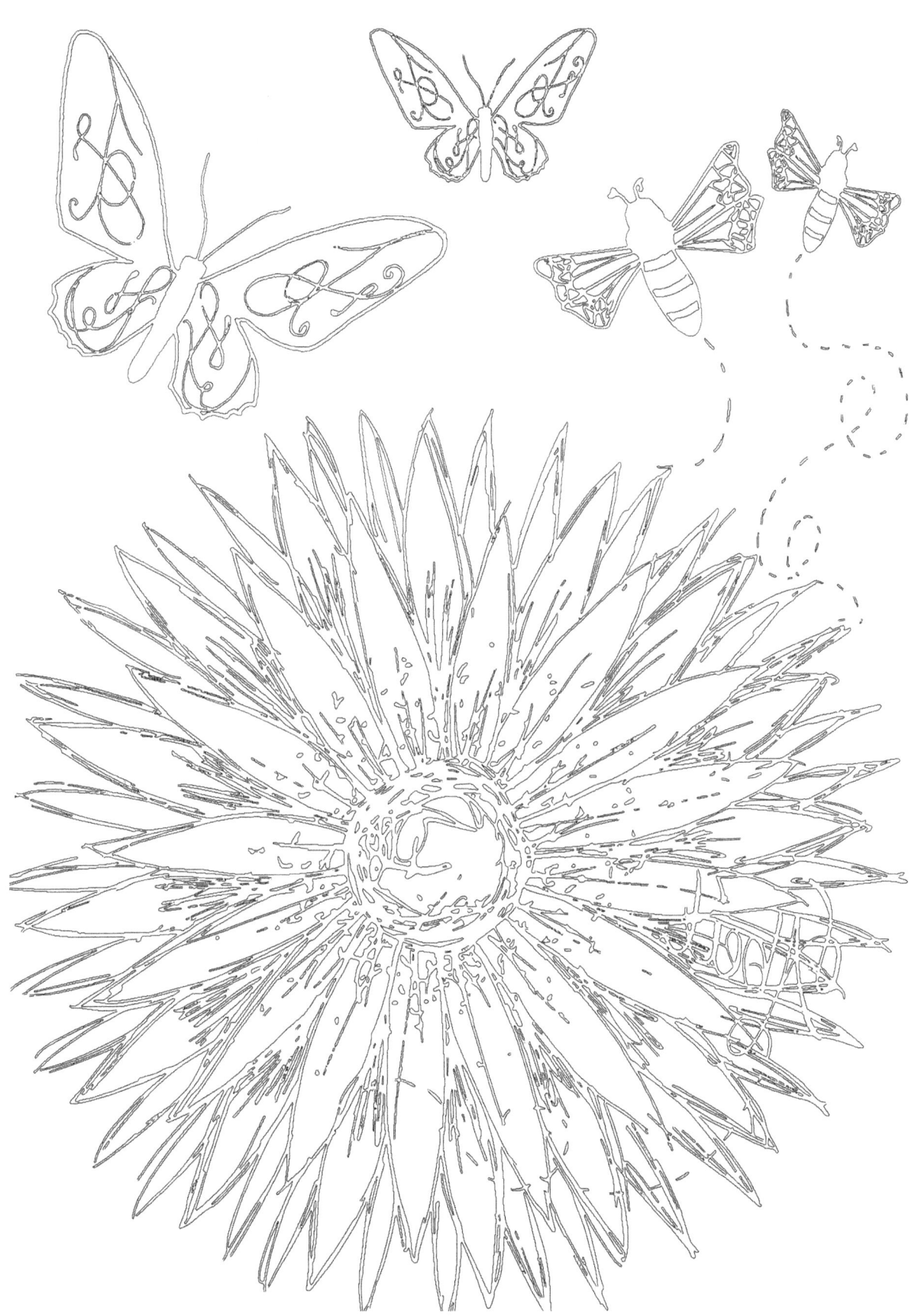

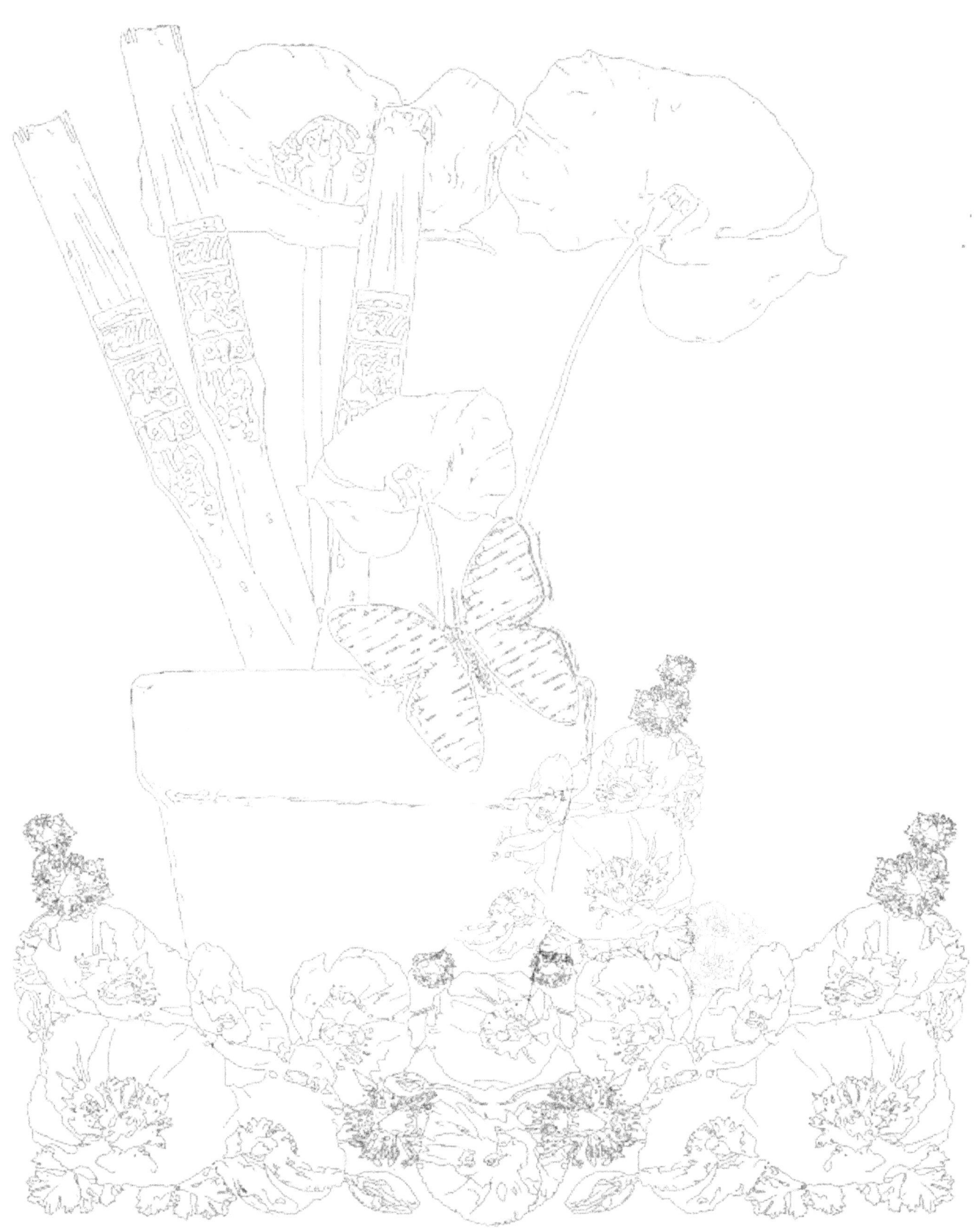

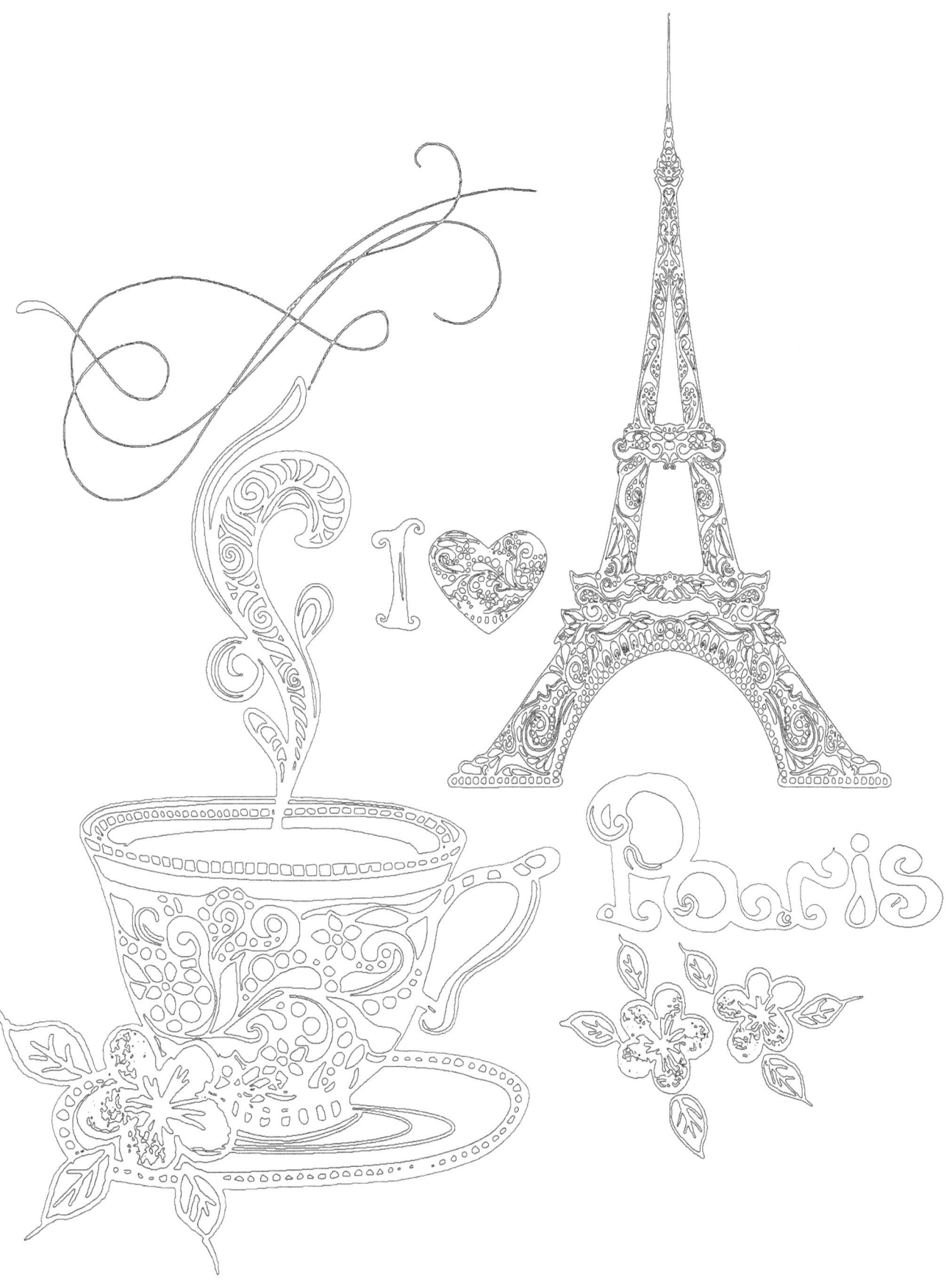

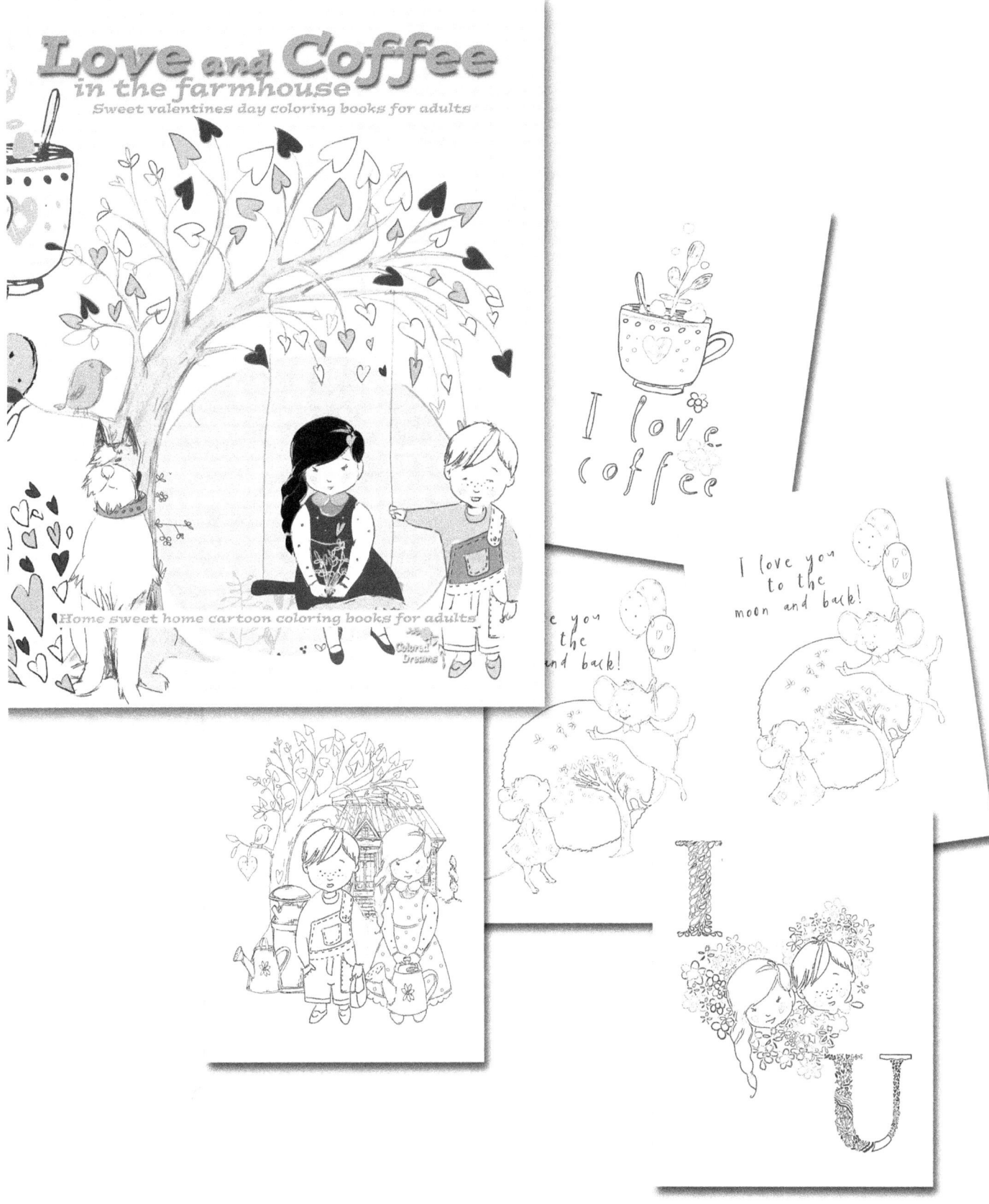

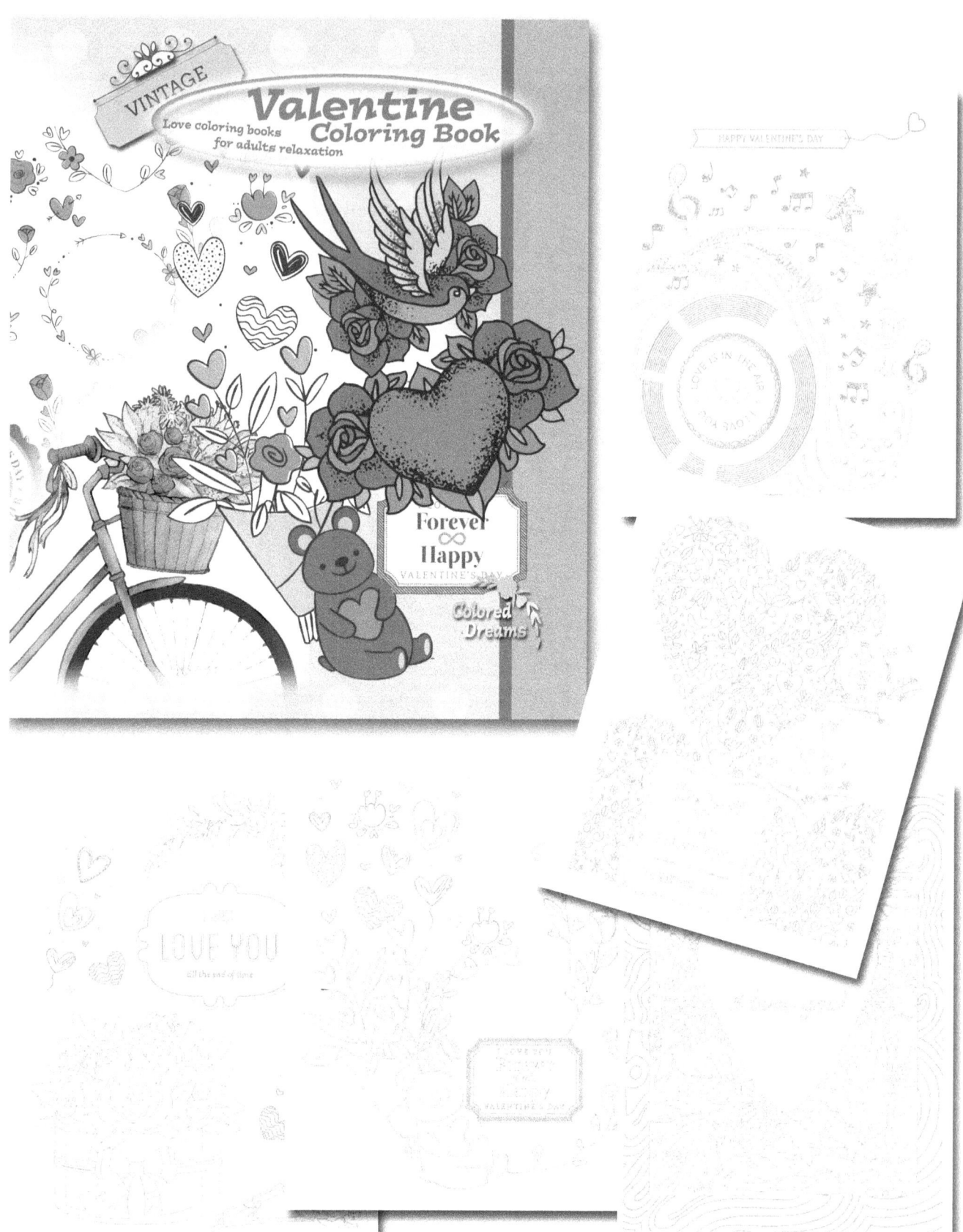

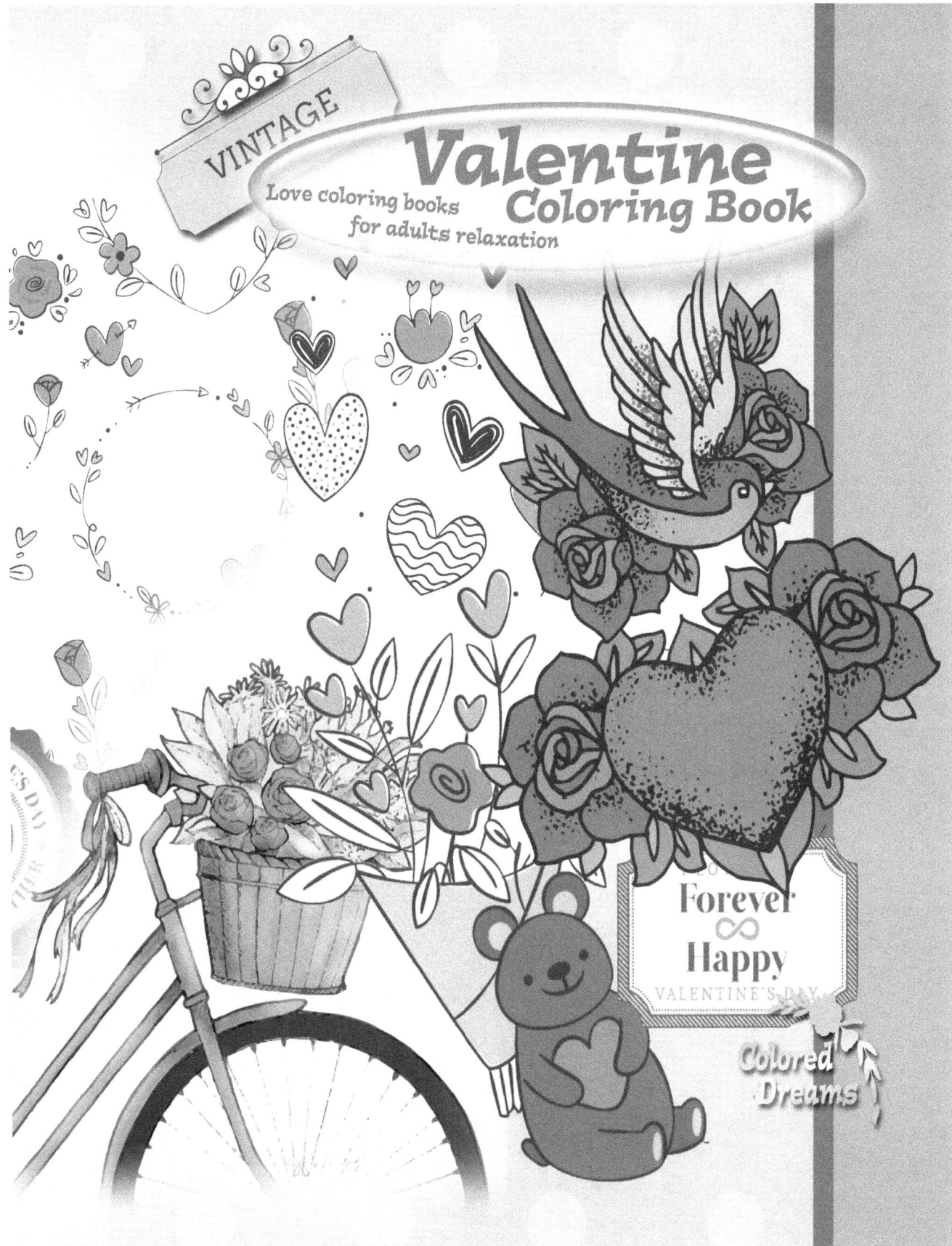

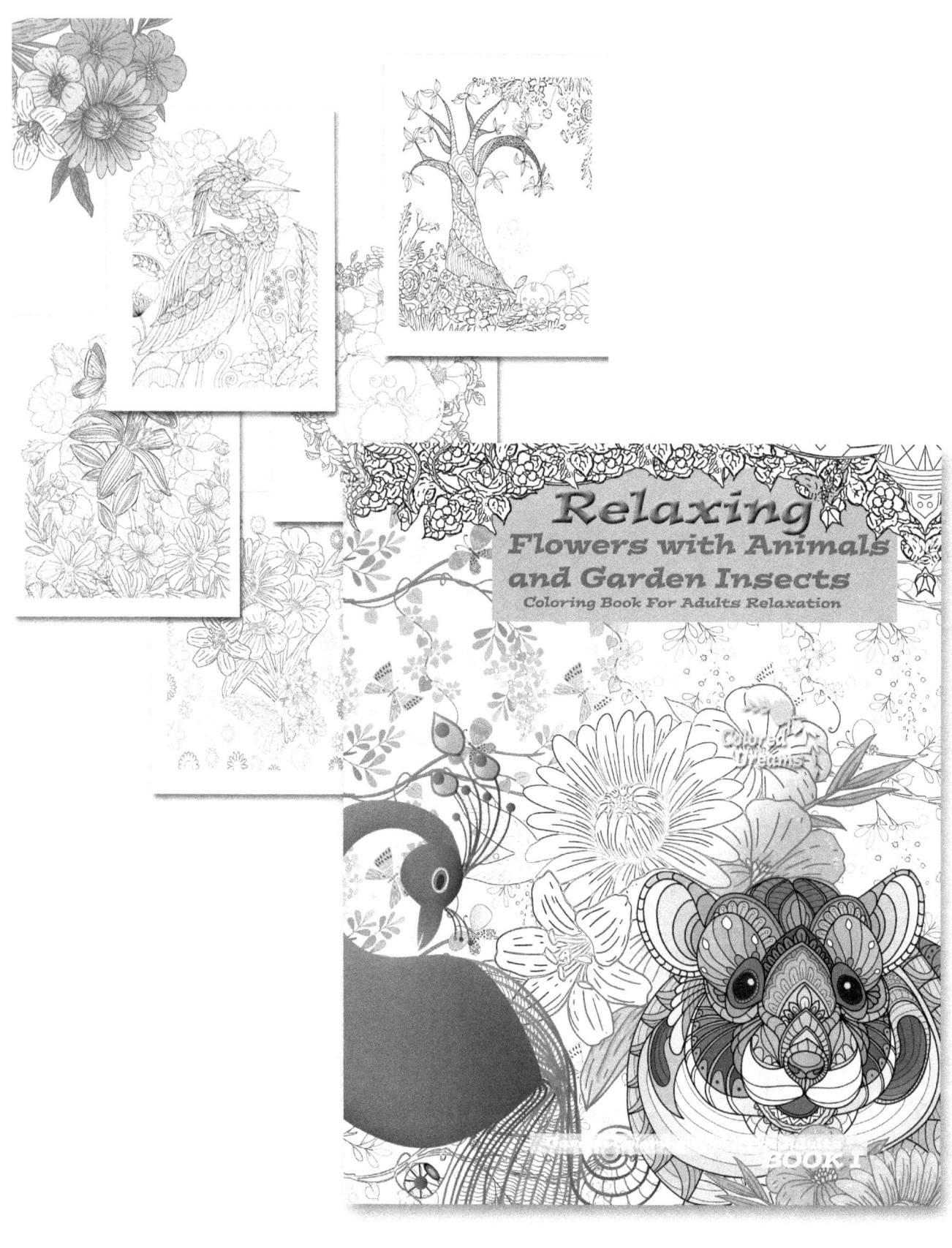

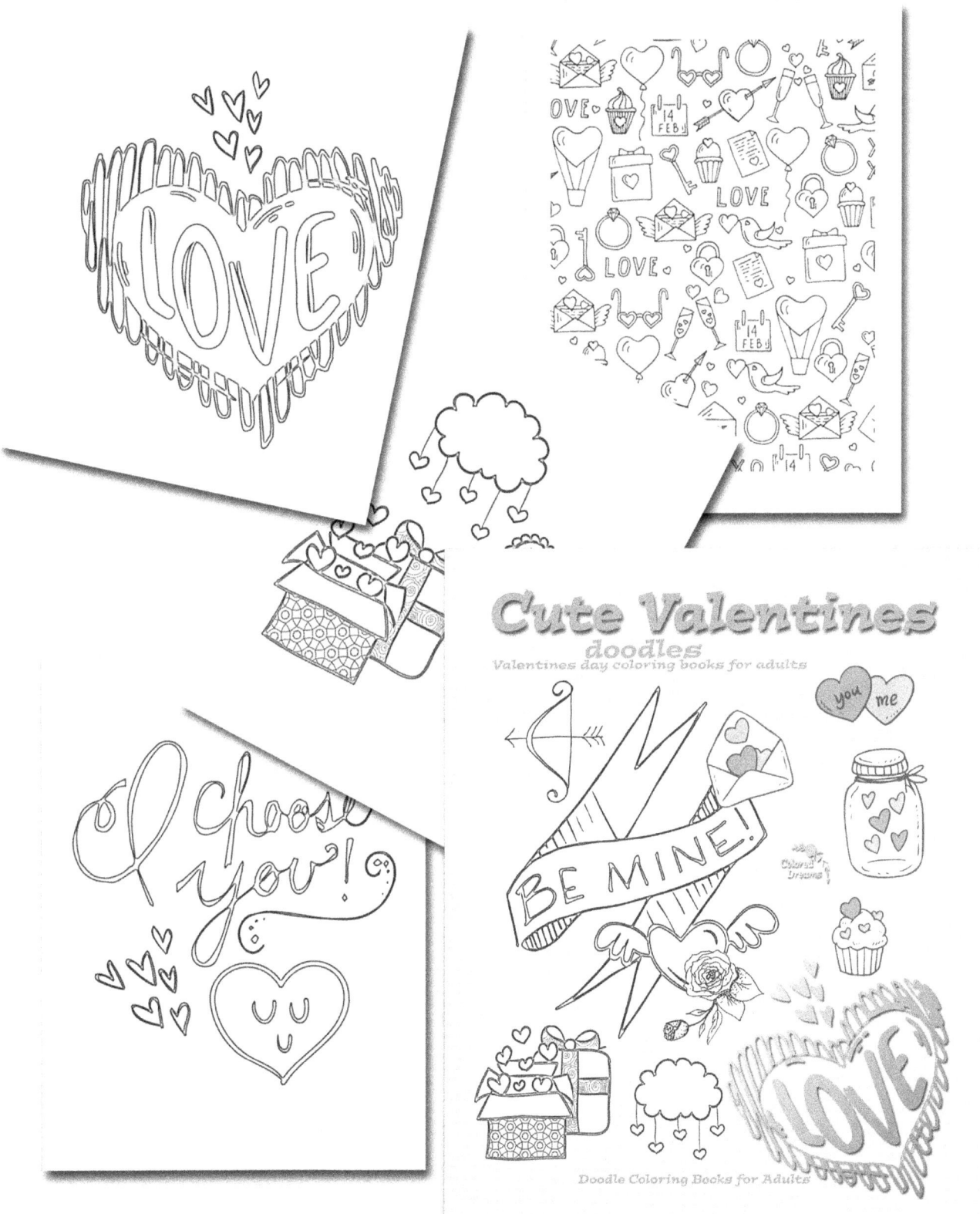

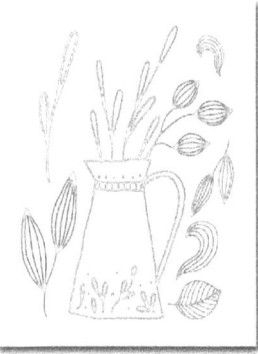
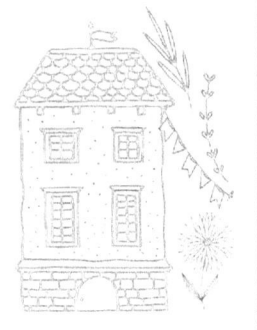
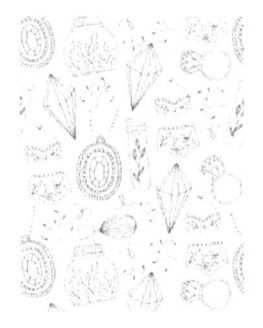
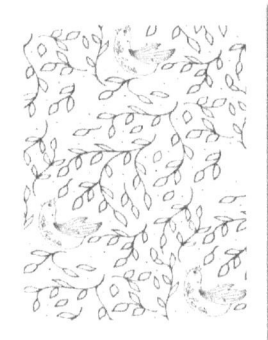
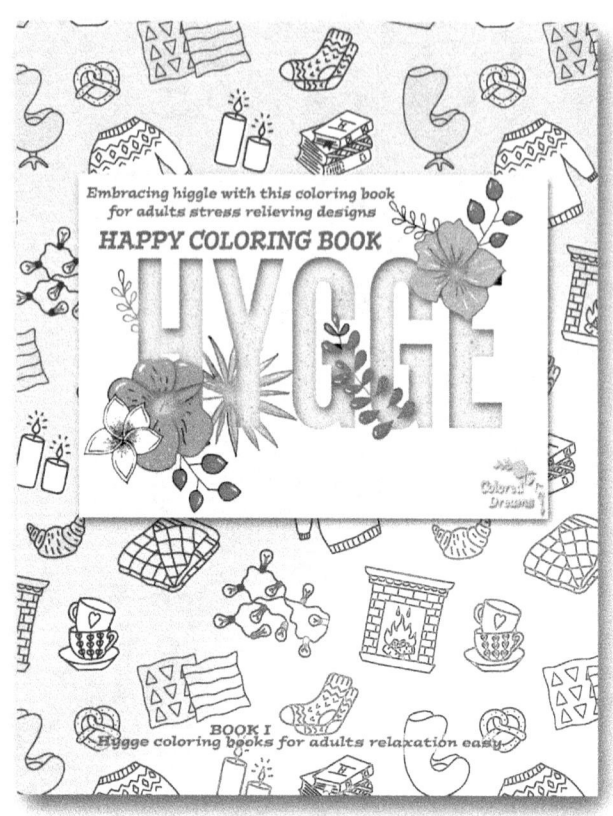
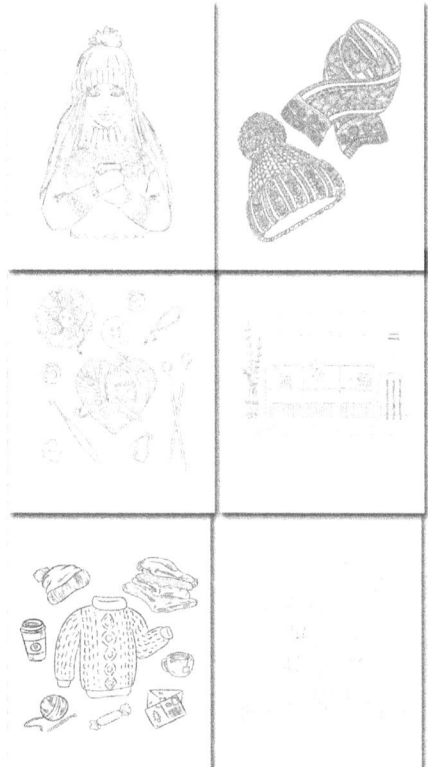
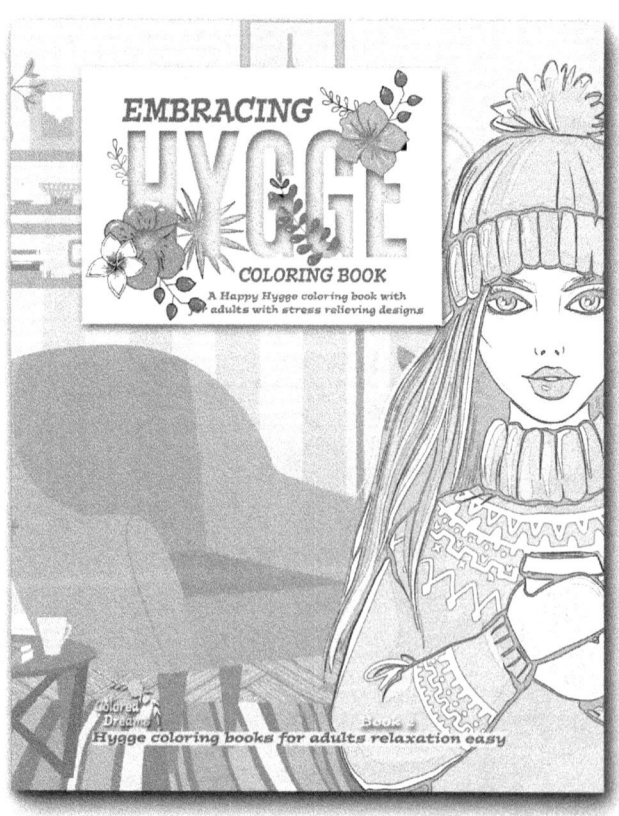

Tag your colored pictures with #vibrantbooks for a change to get your pictures featured on our social media

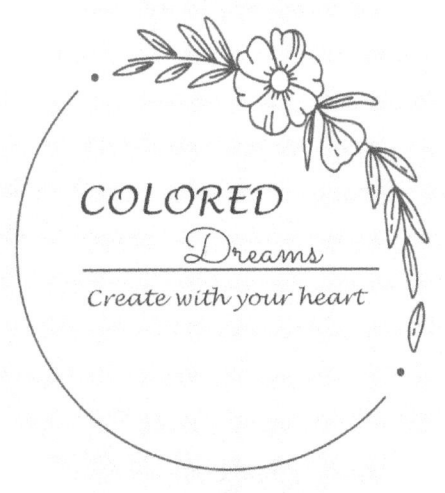

www.ingramcontent.com/pod-product-compliance
Lightning Source LLC
LaVergne TN
LVHW060217080526
838202LV00052B/4292